SILENCE
THE BREAKING OF IT

SHEILA ROSEN

BIG TREE PUBLISHING
LANGLEY, BC

SILENCE—THE BREAKING OF IT
© Sheila Rosen, 2014
All Rights Reserved, except where otherwise noted

Designed by Patrice Nelson

Published by Big Tree Publishing, Langley, BC Canada
ISBN 978-0-9937030-2-7
www.bigtreepublishing.com

DEDICATION

*This book of poems is for my husband, Norm,
whose last words to me when he went out the door
that morning were "full steam ahead".*

ACKNOWLEDGEMENTS

I am grateful for the teaching and inspiration
I've received along the way from:

Regent College (where Luci Shaw first called me a poet)
Burnaby Writers' Society
Writing retreats with Patrick Lane and Richard Osler.

I'm glad and grateful for the encouragement
of my family, too many to name,
and my poet-friends, too many to name.

CONTENTS

TO GO FROM HERE

9   Boundary Creek

10   Old Hotels

11   For Me the Japanese

12   What They Carried

14   The Town Was Long and Thin

15   Nagasaki

16   Bluebirds Over

18   Taking Up the Tracks

19   Nightmare

20   Cotton Dress and My Grandmother's Breasts

21   Child Running

22   Sheila

24   The Moon Came in Winter

25   Road to the Interior

27   To Go from Here

HOW CAN YOU NOT?

31   How Can You Not?

32   Light Wind Coming Downhill

33   Stories in Bed

34   I Have Never Entered This Barn

35   Day of Small Things

36   End of Summer, 2010

37   How I Want

38   Oh Perilous Life

39   Smack

40   Telling

41   I Loves You, Porgy

42   There Must Have Been Wind in the Night

44   Passing a Street

45   Intimations of Grace

47   Ripe Blackberries

48   Without Horses

OR THIS

51   Or This

52   Order/Disorder

54   Clockwork

55   Doing Fractions

56   Main Street and Terminal Avenue,
        waiting for the car to be repaired

58   Snapshot

59   Default: Self Portrait

60   She Comes into Her Own

62   Clear Nights

63   Striped Sea: Random thoughts from the shore

64   Rain Stories

67   Desert Fathers

68   Cloister

TO GO FROM HERE

*There are a thousand thousand reasons to live this life,
everyone of them sufficient.*

Marilynne Robinson, Gilead

Boundary Creek

Near the steel train bridge the creek deepens
for swimming. The chill of mountain water
seeps into young bones. Small bodies shiver.
Girls huddle. Brave and foolish boys lie down
on the hot pavement of number three highway
to thaw.
              There must have been a look-out to yell
car! logging truck! Greyhound bus! I don't
remember that part — only the fearless boys diving
from a weathered wooden foot bridge, and afterward
their slender brown backs blackening in the sun.
And the dark brown creek where the brave girls
waded downstream, turned and lay back to float
looking skyward through tall cottonwoods and
the green willowy overhang, cradled there
as they wondered where, how far,
the current might take them.

Old Hotels

Always going to school we passed
the foundations of old hotels, and old hotels
still standing, never thinking they once were
The Palace, The Alhambra, The Imperial Copper.
Old hotels rendered nameless — now numbered
so the resettled would know they are tracked,
seen to. Number 3, number 5, number 10,
unadorned, minimally furnished, where
school friends and their "enemy alien"
families lived, though I did not learn
and did not hear that naming
anytime in my childhood.

For Me the Japanese

were always there, indigenous as my father
and his grand vegetable-spilling garden, the town
complete and burgeoning, ex-boom-town buildings
spilling bright black-haired children into my life.

In the fillings and emptyings of history
there had been prospectors, miners, entrepreneurs,
then an unsettled waiting for the next filling until
from coastal homes came a people who grieved
ways of life lost, unknown to me.

A child could only see the children and their good luck
to live on the town's main street, right in the middle,
friends just down the way or down the hall, and I
on the outside, walked a mile home from their
chopstick-clicking rice-cooking kitchens,
a mile from their delicious secrets.

What They Carried

Standing now at Amphitrite Point,
I see stolen houses and fishing boats
were not the only theft. This ocean too
was taken and the buoyancy of sea-going.
    Pack all this away in some closet of the mind.
    Draw the curtain. Don't speak of it. Don't say.
    Pack hurriedly into carrying bag or box
    a single keepsake (small), essentials (bare).
The trains lumbered inland, carried them
far enough from the sea for containment
in my narrow circumscribed valley —
how were they able to breathe?
    Pack all this away in some closet of the mind.
    Draw the curtain. Don't speak of it. Don't say.
We didn't think to fathom what they carried
into the dark trains, into our small dying
mining town. Far enough from the sea
for bereavement.
    Draw the curtain. Don't speak of it. Don't say.

After many years they spoke — of returning.
Why would they leave me, leave our town
for some place called Ucluelet? The Pacific
still smashes into rocks at Amphitrite Point.
Breakers splinter into white cataracts,
what we didn't know they carried
into the interior.

      Draw the curtain. Don't say.

The Town was Long and Thin

The town was long and thin; inclined
to hug the highway, the creek, close hills.
Beside the creek, twin crab-apple trees
bloomed, as they do, side by side. Two girls
fastened blossoms in their hair. One fly-away
red, the other thick black. Coarse hair, fine hair,
words grown-ups used. Two girls skipped rope,
then faster, 'til the flowers slipped to the path
worn hard by wheelbarrows pushed from house
to garden to house through growing seasons.
One girl's father had plied the sea for fish.
Now he plied dry forests for fir and pine;
sailed the waves of dust on narrow
logging roads. Somewhere far
away from the long thin town,
the war had ended.

Nagasaki

We meant to go to Hiroshima, but Nagasaki
turned out to be more convenient. I should have
insisted. I meant to go to Hiroshima but they said
one epicentre's as good as another. I wanted
to go to Hiroshima. It happened, you see, on my
sixth birthday. We had a little party on the lawn.
The Kitagawa children came. Sometimes I talk about
Hiroshima as if I've been there, toured the museum,
but I've only been to Nagasaki. They meant to
drop their Fat Man on Kokura on the third day after
Hiroshima, but cloud-cover prevented. Nagasaki
turned out to be more convenient, as the clouds
parted over Urakami valley, opening a window
for their Fat Man. A small Japanese lady told us,
delicately, "a bomb fell there." It did, with irony,
on cosmopolitan Nagasaki, Japan's open window
on the world, centre for Japanese Christianity,
home to Urakami Cathedral — sacrament
of penance and reconciliation about to begin
when "a bomb fell there." A few rosaries, a few
blackened stone saints found, an angelus bell
made in France. It's always our own we are
at war with; Hiroshima, Nagasaki, always, only,
bombing ourselves, one epicentre as good as another.

Bluebirds Over

There's a map in my mind of a rural house.
You enter at the back door, follow green mottled linoleum
room to room 'til you reach the fir-floored front hall
and a stairway to the partial second storey.
Dormer windows north and south, make one cruciform-shaped
room to which my brother Jim returned, for old times' sake,
when he was seventy-five and dying.

I'm told he cried (which he was not wont to do)
in this room where he and his siblings once slept,
dreamed. *The White Cliffs of Dover* sheet music
was on the piano downstairs, when Jim left
to "join up," Mother at the piano, singing "and Jimmy
will go to sleep in his own little room again . . ."

The war ended before he was sent *over there*,
but he spent his whole air force life navigating,
circumnavigating the world, surviving plane crashes
(once on an Arctic ice floe). Close call,
nine lives like a cat.

Still he was the first to go. We scattered his ashes
on the shiny black slag from the old smelter
where he used to play, and some were scattered
in the creek into which he threw the turnips
he was "harvesting" — he wanted to see if they'd
float like wood *"because that's what they taste like"*
and the rest of his ashes we placed in an urn,
buried it by our parents' graves with tall pines
and bluebirds over, and peace ever . . .
for Jimmy to go to sleep.

Taking Up the Tracks

They've taken up the tracks where once
the train came daily, announcing itself
with whistles and grand belches of steam
to locals waiting on the platform to ride
to the big town twenty-eight miles east, a town
with a dentist; even little kids sometimes making
that journey alone; and the woman in the tweed coat
and maroon felt hat standing at the maroon station
waving goodbye as she headed west to Vancouver
and what would turn out to be a double mastectomy
and the Japanese arriving en masse and the Catholic
sisters of the Atonement there to comfort, and the mayor
and police and Security Commission meeting the train
to ensure good order as if the Japanese knew nothing
about order, and a time years later when the Japanese
would be allowed to climb of their own free will back
on the trains and leave us there, diminished, as the trains
too diminished and in time the grand and great grand
children of the lady with the double mastectomy would
bicycle the rail bed for recreation and a need
not fully understood to recreate the story,
the tie that runs through them
like a line of steel.

Nightmare

She hears through the wall
her father's snore. She prepares
for bed and listens for the frantic shout
as he struggles to surface, to scramble up
from underground before everything
caves in and smothers him. When it comes
she goes to his room to pull him free.

Morning, she sees his bed is made,
his miner's lamp gone from the hook
and she knows he is already
hours underground.

Cotton Dress and My Grandmother's Breasts

When my grandmother showed me
her shrivelled breasts, I was wearing
a dress of green plaid Dan River cotton.

My older sister had measured my bust
at the fullest part; waist at narrowest;
hips at broadest; length of bodice
measured down the spine, intimate
assessment of my shy body.

Deft, diligent, she drafted a pattern
on newspaper, pinned, cut, basted
— the cotton still carrying that happy
new-material smell of the dry-goods store.

By the time I visited Grandma in my Dan River dress
I was beginning to strain the buttons a bit, but wouldn't
give up my favourite dress. And Grandma had already
run onto the highway in her nightgown (or was it without
her nightgown?) Other stunts too indicating dementia.
Now pulling me close to her bed, she whispered,
"I used to have nice breasts like you, but see,"
she fingered the small crumpled sacs,
"it's better to be young."

Child Running

Child running
           in every direction
the path drops
           into abyss
in every direction,
           sink-holes
pock-marking
           the fields.

Persistent nightmare
Child waking, saved by battleship linoleum,
mottled green, durable, firm underfoot.

I know something I didn't then,
how tectonic plates grind and slip, jockeying
for the upper hand, abyss a possibility.

This knowledge is from science,
therefore bound to be truer than
the surety of mottled green linoleum.

All summer, we played jacks
on the bedroom floor. I know this,
remember how perfectly solid and level
and smooth under our clever hands,
how pleasingly cool against our child thighs
was the green linoleum when we came in
from running in the dry rock-strewn fields.
Is remembering the same as knowing?

Sheila

(a fictitious, mythical, or real person after whom this poem is named and to whom it refers eponymously)

Liking the word eponymous,
I title my poem Sheila. Now,
it seems, I must go on (and on) about
me — last child of ten my mother bore,
first one born in hospital and so
a thoroughly modern Sheila.

Cellar door cut into kitchen floor,
eggs in waterglass in a crock
down the steep stairs — dare
to put your hands into its slime.
Dank earth smell. Eerily sprouting
potatoes. Wide-mouth Masons.
Storm windows. Long stockings.
Weather stripping. Outhouse.
Hunting rifles. Bear grease for
leather boots. Wood piles. Peevee.
Cross-cut saw. Miner's lamp. Ice blocks
in sawdust. Hand-cranked ice-cream
maker. Bannister to slide down.
Shed roofs to jump off, thinking
I might fly. And we had a car!

A maroon Hudson — pop-up regular
on the pages of my past. Where
did he get that thing? My Dad.

My Mother, calling me Lady Jane,
Sheila girl; calling the train engineer
who didn't wave back, a piker.
Every morning, heading to the barn
by the little brown creek to milk
our one cow. Her same strong fingers
on the piano playing Robin's Return.
Sheet music: *I'm going to buy*
a Paper Doll that I can call my own . . .

Ssh, Sheila, ssh, listen — war news
from the Marconi on the corner cupboard.
Finally it was over. Finally, cancer.

Shy Sheila, hiding under the bed
from brothers home in uniform,
running to escape fearsome cameras,
watching from a corner of the room,
listening. No answer for the teasing
uncles, brothers, others — the cat
always having my tongue.

The Moon Came in Winter

The moon came in winter
to our narrow valley
where timbered hills delayed
the sun, hurried the dark.
The moon came in winter
to the colourless lay of land;
did not despise the smallness
that smothered us there to sleep;
brought, if not colour, brightness.
The weary snow quickened,
shivered down our spines, and we
began to breathe again. There are gifts
that help you through those nights
tilted away from the sun.

Road to the Interior

And some time make the time to drive out west
Into County Clare, along the Flaggy Shore.
Seamus Heaney, *Postscript*

Seamus says drive west. I go east,
to the Monashees, interior hills
that once wrapped me, then
sent me packing at sixteen.

I'm the girl; I'm the aging poet
coming into dry country. My interior
voices like rain-splash on dusty roads.
Hard water, hard rock mining, Dad
mucking back. Copper, silver,
gold, galena. Phoenix, Deadwood,
Anaconda. Ghost towns. Mine shafts
we were not to go near. The Slag Dump
we were not to play on but did
for its moon-scape surface, its black
massiveness, looming over the small
brown creek. So easy to slip over
its slaggy smooth edge.
Passing the chamois-cloth hillsides

of Midway (midway to where?)
I follow Boundary Creek, past
where we picked watercress, past
the Falls, past the falling barns turned
mouse-grey. I'm the girl. I'm the lover
of old barns, old poets. Seamus,
born in that Ireland the year I was born
in this Canada. And him gone now.
Through the open window a meadowlark
buoyant on barbed wire.

I'm collecting empties along the roadside's
raggy shore, draining their last liquory stories.
Past the road that heads up Norwegian Creek,
the failed farm, its hardships told in dribs.
And them gone now, who might tell more.
I stay on highway three to Greenwood.
Greenwood: who would I know, who
would know me, now, on this road
to the interior? Neither here
nor there, nor sixteen.

To Go from Here

This hamlet, this long thin town,
this circumscribed valley
is the gift I was given:
an opening sentence,
a first line.

HOW CAN YOU NOT?

... but it's your existence I love you for, mainly. Existence seems to me now the most remarkable thing that could ever be imagined.

Marilynne Robinson, *Gilead*

How Can You Not?

When a djeli *passed away, the knowledge of*
one-hundred men died with him.
Lawrence Hill, *The Book of Negroes*

How can you not be drawn
to a man whose curiosity
is a hungry mouth;
how not admire
this lust;
how not mourn
the slipping away
of his stories, his know-how,
the strength of his hands
their generosity;
how can you not be in love
with a man who rides horses?

Light Wind Coming Downhill

Light wind lifting
my copper-coloured hair.
You're the one who called it
shining, called it copper,
who plunged into it,
who plied my body's divide,
supple fingers signifying
kisses up and down
my spine.
You're the wind, the light wind
coming down the hill, down
the rolling hill, down the green,
down the lilting grassy hill.
You're the wind brushing
my copper hair. You're
the light wind
lifting.

Stories in Bed

(after Robert Hass)

In the field behind the house, he said,
there were always old apple trees,
their splayed craggy arms propped up,
still yielding the sweetest apples.
Outside the fence, up over the hill,
the grass was greenest; and winters,
he said, on Sunday afternoons,
they would toboggan or take turns
on long wooden skis.
Now, her stories take her into sleep,
or not: it's the same hill —
lying down together on the soft grass,
unseen — just over the rise
from the farmhouse — that was before
they married — then how was it
so soon — their children,
their grandchildren — walking up the hill —
old farmhouse gone now —
the children — their small handfuls of ashes —
the wind — carrying his stories away.

I Have Never Entered This Barn

I have never entered this barn
with its liquid windows.
Hard glass, it seems, is fluid.
It slumps. You don't believe it
and neither does the dead robin
who only wanted to find
the fluid sky. This window
has been here since the barn began.
See how it's running down,
how it thickens toward the sill?

I have never entered this barn
but the farmer's son every day
of his young life has gone in.
The farmer's son knows new hay,
old straw, every mouse nest,
manure, worn saddles, warm milk,
the stomp of the cows in the stall,
slivers of barn board under the nails.
The farmer's son sees through
the waves of the old window
something out there,
something skewed.

Sloping away from the barn
there is a long road.

Day of Small Things

Who despises the day of small things? Zechariah 4:10

Again this morning, I woke up
alive, so I have another, maybe not
momentous — humdrum will do.

A day of little wind, only a few gusts
of annoyance, a missing sprinkler
and the garden grows thirsty. The sky-blue
hydrangea droops in a sulk. Its name
means *water vessel* and it wants to be filled.
I'll hand-water. I have time.

In the humdrum house — a fan
oscillates benediction — a priest
sprinkling holy water right and left.
Heat enervates. Only small tasks
will be done (thy will be done
on earth as in heaven.)

Do not despise the day
nor the smallness of things.
Any humdrum day might turn
momentous — someone leaves
and does not return.

End of Summer, 2010

How is summer already shot
as from a cannon last May
and now this hard landing.

I have a rendezvous
with darkness. Fear's the thing,
of loneliness I know

will infiltrate through cold
winter windows — impermeable
to rain but not to that.

All summer I had the light
for solace; now it, too, takes
its leave. Stubborn tilted planet!

Nights will be long and without
the familiar muttering ourselves
off to bed. Did you remember

the back door and the lights?
Has the fireplace cooled? You left
your glasses by the tub.

How I Want

How I want
to grieve is to lean
against the hard chest
of a man. My flesh
disintegrating, dissolving
into the other's solidity.

How I want
to retrieve the density
of his body, the way it was
when he was newly sprung
from his boyhood on the ranch
work-wiry and muscled.
Hardness, softness,
gifts for each other.

Oh Perilous Life

I've got your number. You're
strong drink. You lavish and delight.
You take away; you tear away.
Benign ruler. Tyrant.

Benefactor. Thief.
Does the sea never cease
heaving in its grief. Will it not quit!
Not only in nightmares
do torn bridal gowns hang
from twisted trees; do words
smash heads against walls.

You want more than I can give,
hard-working heart always
in the dark, my sternum
never having been split
for corrective surgery.
Can light get in?

Oh! Perilous life, I know
how swift, how smart,
how searing, how sweet
is your passage.

Smack

The varied thrush smacked hard glass
and fell on the frozen reflecting pool.
I contemplated his v-patterned vest,
his splayed wings in their still beauty.

When my husband hit the hardwood floor
he lay still under frantic efforts to revive him,
I'm told his vital signs gave momentary flutterings,
like the thrush, but he continued frozen
in this sudden surprise ending.

At the viewing, his vest was etched velvet,
handmade, shades of purple, a gift
I'd given him for his love of all things
bright and beautiful.

For this reason I cried long
and unreasonably
for the thrush.

Telling

(almost a sonnet)

*I think we delight to praise what we enjoy because
the praise not merely expresses but completes the
enjoyment; it is its appointed consummation.*
C.S. Lewis, *Reflections on the Psalms*

Solitude and seasons don't go well
together. Now I live and walk alone
through tulip spring and leafy fall
and know, alone, my summer's flown
away to winter, the bite and chill
of every season brings me down
and every spirited wind's a knell
that rings a prophesying sound
as when a storm-tossed gull
tells the anxious seaside town
he's gone, he's gone. I'll dwell
in solitude through seasons now
and no old friend will hear me tell
my praise for all I see and know
of heaven here below.

I Loves You, Porgy*

I have become like a bird alone on a roof. Psalm 102:7

Sometimes I catch myself singing
I loves you, Porgy — just that line.
What else is there — I loved you;
now you're gone it seems
I loves you more.
That fierce interval separating the two
syllables in "Por-gy" — just three semi-tones,
but so hard to reach the high G unless
I fly up to that higher rooftop —
a fiddler, a singer, the two of us,
and I no longer a bird alone
on a hard tile roof.

*From the opera *Porgy and Bess* by George & Ira Gershwin

There Must Have Been Wind
in the Night

At six a.m. I picked up the paper
from my doorstep and stepped
farther out just to feel the dark.
Stars were brighter than expected
in a city sky; Venus was beaming.
There must have been wind in the night
clearing away the particulate.
I'd already seen what might have been
a bright satellite, or maybe just a plane,
traversing my bedroom skylight.

Now it was coming to me — last night's
dream — and it was the young sailor
I sat beside on a Greyhound bus
when I was seventeen, too shy to talk
we held hands from town to town until
we arrived at mine and I stepped off,
leaving him, his face pressed against
the bus window, and me, alone,
on the sidewalk by the Windsor Hotel.

He sailored on to some place farther
into the Interior. His town, his face,
lost to me in the full fifty-five years
I've lived since, that's how long ago

it was, mere wisp of memory — *once
there was this sailor on a bus,
waving goodbye.* Last night he arrived
in my dream, still young,
and I, old and alone, kissed him.

Passing a Street

I thought about loneliness today,
passing a street I once lived on in that estate.
Street of old widowed landladies, narrow beds,
plain rooms. It was an early dis-location —
despair, unnamed, of ever finding affinity or place.
Mrs. Geary told me her life: England, India,
Canada. I was young when I lived a winter
on that street and didn't listen well enough,
but it was enough, for her, just to tell.

Variations:
The estate of loneliness by neglect is not the same
as by betrayal — the one an un-replenished cupboard;
the other, mouse droppings on all the shelves;
loneliness by abandonment is not the same
as by death — the one an empty closet, stripped;
the other an old plaid shirt you keep. It keeps
you warm and makes you weep with wishing
and remembering — until you utter little cries
of praise, regret, thanksgiving, even laughter.

Intimations of Grace

When the chickadee rings
the Indian brass bell
suspended from a twisted wisteria
over the small pond where birds
are fond of bathing;

and a butterfly flits frailly
in and out of the light blue
hydrangea, where I sit and read
Between Noon and Three
by Robert Farrar Capon
and it is, between noon and three
of a late August afternoon;

when the pinnate shadows
of wisteria leaves rustle
full of grace on terracotta tiles;
and the subject of my reading
is the outrage of grace;
and piano music, Chopin,
(live concert from Warsaw)
plays from above the glass patio table,
(speaker well-placed by my husband,

while he lived, loving music);
and in Warsaw, the Polish Chopin
lovers wildly applaud their own;
when the miracle of a jet plane,
flashing overhead, flies away
from itself; and in a small outrage
of grace, someone agrees
to go out in the heat to fetch
French Vanilla ice-cream,

then *"it is meet that we
should make merry, and be glad,*
for weren't we all, at some time,
dead and are alive, lost and are found."

Ripe Blackberries

We visited the elders, their ways —
at once old and other and familiar.
Spoons, scrapers, bowls, bent boxes —
handled, sacred and suitable.

And time
seemed to us an animal
we could not tame and should not try to tame.

We couldn't
take it in. We went out
to the promontory by the museum.
A bench was there, maybe for prayer.

Through the trees, the Pacific, and it was
the same sea — and what was its name,
when a young Musqueam or an Elder
might have walked there, right there,
or sat, or crouched, or gathered?

And time, the animal, crouched there with me.
And my husband, the wanderer, went exploring
and returned with handfuls from a thicket, seeping
red from black into his brown beautiful hands;
"they're ripe" he said, "take, eat."

Without Horses

a world that cannot be crossed without horses
Federico García Lorca

My children fatherless, before long
motherless. They're not young;
I can go; they have their own. Generation
follows generation across a world
that cannot be crossed without horses.

Where are the horses, then?
The wagons are laden. How
will they cross the world? How
will the logs be skidded,
the sod turned by the plow?

And are there no horses
for the cortege? And who
are these ones gathering, these ones
walking behind the coffin; how
will they cross over without horses?

OR THIS

This is an interesting planet.
It deserves all the attention you can give it.

Marilynne Robinson, *Gilead*

Or This

Sometimes through a glass darkly
I see this:

some great incendiary mind
shovelling coal into the firebox;
keeping the system running pretty much
on time. Departures. Arrivals. Already
he's laid tracks through mountain passes;
he's the engineer in striped engineer's cap,
the conductor, ticketer, stoker, stoking,
ever stoking the fire.

or this:
some great flammable heart
wanting to set mine afire,
always wanting me to see
possibility, ever imagining

this,
or maybe this,
or this.

Order/Disorder

(one)
Here's a way of seeing it: in the beginning
a diminution.

God pulling back to let not-God
come to be. Simone Weil calls it contraction,
suffering.

You might say God
broke off a piece of himself;
parted with it.

What did he let go — something small,
wafer-thin? Or a sizeable basin of starter —
yeasty, bubbling, transubstantiated

from god-ness to thing-ness, with all
attendant symmetries, bifurcations, fractals,
ripe for the making of a well-behaved universe —
ordered and, with due diligence on our part,
readable, unlike himself?

(two)
Order becomes us.
In our beginning was our need
for places to hold us and our matter.
A hide tent or small stone surround
to keep us from spillage, from disarray.

We needed sorting and stashing spaces
and small cracked places in walls
to push prayers into.

Elaborating, we riffed on ancient orders
for approaching the ineffable — arched,
angled, circular, cruciform frameworks.
We believed (rightly?) God to be
a fan of whatsoever is of good design.
A fan who'd not eschew the beautiful,
the stunning; would not look askance
at alabaster windows; who'd delight,
as do we, in the symmetry of rotundas,
their painted domes; still a fan who knows
we are sawdust — all chisels, nails,
hammers, thumbs.

(three)
Incautiously we ask God
to bring his unruly self into our prim
meeting houses, basilicas, amphitheatres,
chapels, stone circles; into small cracked places
in crumbling rock walls; all unremarked interstices
into which we press our formal folded requests and,
our disorderly bellowings and wailings.

Clockwork

In war's midnight realm
when guns and bombs might,
for a while, be quieted, fear still
comes, a hungry clockwork ghost,
ticking its way up and down
the silent street. Memory
does not let go of slaughter;
does not let go of the innocent
hungry children, the gift of them
all undone in war's clockwork
disassembly line.

Doing Fractions

We are one cell perpetually dying, and being born,
led by a single day that presides over our passage through
the thirty thousand days from highchair past work and love
to suffering death. Donald Hall, *The One Day*

If longevity is our lot, one over thirty thousand
is the fraction we work with any given day.
(In this arithmetic, there are no proofs.) Bombs
are going off all the time — in airplanes, arteries,
cells — diminishing our denominator.

The integer we work toward is one:
natural and whole. But we are refracted,
factored, broken down, extended
in all directions. The relationship this present
numerator bears to the whole is lost.

Wanted: pure mathematician — rational,
basic, to help us calculate values,
the quotidian fractions, proper and positive,
the sum of which will give the answer,
our cardinal number: one

Main Street and Terminal Avenue, waiting for the car to be repaired

Outside the coffee shop, the young
in love, laughing. He lifts a swirl of her hair,
kisses the place where first responders
feel for a pulse. So young to know
to kiss her there.

Inside, two guys talk Japan. How so young
do they know all this; how so articulate?
I want to say, "include me." I've seen it too:
Congested Kyoto cemetery. One of two
A-bomb epicentres. Long skeins of hand-dyed
silk stretched to dry. Exquisite art, manners;
excruciating expectations.

Memory's eccentricity — in Florence, it was
Michelangelo's four unfinished sculptures
held me on the way to David, hold me still.
Venice: wooden sidewalk sections piled up
in Piazza San Marco, waiting for the flood.
New York: a kind of déjà vu — the familiar
movie world of a small-town childhood —
every Saturday night at the Jewel Theatre.

Desire, lust even, for another try, another crack
at the marble with my unskilled chisel. To live,
this time, closer to the core, authentic as Christ;
to die, like him, for being so perfectly what I am.

I am in love with this world, see it racing away
to court the young. Thou shalt not covet.
Jealous, I want to be starting out like these:
the one with his back to me — British accent,
likely at home in at least two countries.
Or the dark expressive friend, accent
as yet undeciphered. Or the two outside,
holding hands now, running for the bus.
Young, laughing gods.

Snapshot

Unknown Young Man, Ireland,
jacket photograph, Seamus Heaney's
District and Circle. Time trickling
or streaming, doesn't come to a full stop.
But the snap of a shot might come closest
to surcease, what we seem to want, warily.

Unknown young man, Ireland,
stands outdoors in his three-piece suit
one hand on an "AGITATOR," forged
in the Philip Pierce & Co. Foundry, Wexford.
I don't know Wexford, or what the machine
agitated (possibly turnips) and though I've
seen things, there are many I've missed,
like Ireland and the inside of a foundry.

Unknown young man, Ireland,
an arresting sepia suspension, causes
a small shift and I see there was
a then which is also always, where
an Irishman and a photographer
stopped the onrush and this picture
could be me or you or my father or yours.
Snapshots hoard passing nows, interfere
at times with now's now; now is always
on its way past, becoming then
or forever or never.

Default: Self Portrait

Albrecht Dürer, thirteen, took silverpoint
to paper, drawing what he could discern
of himself. Genius already bearing down.
A tender, skillful rendering, first of many
selves he would commit: Dürer
at twenty-two, Dürer at twenty-six.
Dürer, twenty-eight, looking like Christ.

See also Rembrandt: Rembrandt at easel,
Rembrandt as beggar, Rembrandt wide-eyed,
Rembrandt as St. Paul. Likewise Van Gogh:
Vincent with pipe, Vincent with straw hat,
Vincent with pipe *and* straw hat.
Gauguin: self-portrait on tobacco jar,
self-portrait with halo, even
Agony in the Garden: Christ,
looking like Gauguin.

World, body, self. The recurring shove
of the self is from world back to body.
Our eyes are fingertips inquiring
of our skin, the way a blind man
learns a face. We stare at our own
indecipherable stare. Can't catch ourselves
not looking. Even a blurred murky mirror
draws us. We blurt out Gauguin's questions:
Where do we come from? What are we?
Where are we going?

She Comes into Her Own

All day cliché, cynicism, sophism, cool-ism
work against delight; discomfort her,
lean toward nihilism, everything seeming
plastic or metallic. Then the 5 pm bus is all
metal and hot plastic as she slumps her head
on the sill. Riders drain into the depot. Her brain,
bloggy, overheated, is ineffectual in an effort
to empty itself at the end of the line.

She comes into her own dwelling. Cool
terracotta tiles ease sweaty feet. Clean,
non-ironic comfort seeps slowly, sub-
liminally in through extremities. Home's
where you hang out — you and your hat;
where you don't hang yourself out to dry,
she murmurs not noticing her hangover
of cliché. Her humidifier/dehumidifier
(purchase of great price) offers deep breathing
space, reassures as an old friend might do
(but hasn't of late).

                    Her head is clearing
room for reflection. Notions, big ones,

slide in: Body/*versus*/Spirit versus
Body/*and*/Spirit; the likelihood of Time
ever coming to an end; or not. Thoughts click
on pathways implicit in a list of isms
she once visited; her mind opens up theism
versus deism: is or isn't God hanging out,
maybe here, doing whatever it is he does? Possibly
ripening the two tomatoes on the windowsill?
Take your time, girl. No hurry to figure this out.
She runs cold water over curly lettuces, carves
bell peppers into green and yellow parentheses,
slivers a few small commas of purple onion,
then a scatter of cilantro. Oh . . . the lightness
of being allowed slow thinking, no fast pat
answers. Just the slow curving of colour and cool
into the body; the pleasures of dwelling.

Clear Nights

Look at the night's excitable stars — a busy life,
star life, seeding the universe with possible worlds.
Possible, I think, stars are fond of our clear nights
preferring to play to an audience — expanding,
contracting, collapsing (perhaps into laughter).

Look at them, circus performers defying gravity
by working it to their advantage, making stars
of themselves; trapeze artists of the galaxies;
clowns with carnival secrets up their sleeves
winking at Earth and her meandering siblings.

You can see, this clear night, it's not the pale moon
that excites me — no, it's the incomprehensible
magnitude and distance of stars and the surprising
nearness of Mars, Venus — bright wanderers, elusive,
not telling all, like the truth reflected in the mirror

above my vanity. I know sin (surely
the most despised word in modernity) is real,
but tonight under the exuberance of the big top,
I'm swayed to believe in a possible world
seeded with grace, and the nearness of you.

Striped Sea:
Random thoughts from the shore

The sea's quick-change stripes
sail out from shore in shades of indigo.
By the time they touch the sky,
they're strips of silver.

The language of waves wants
a gift of interpretation. Bach
made a stab at it, a good one.
His indigo fugues, passions, partitas
cut into me like Scripture.

I'm a short piece of sacred
choral music, contrapuntal,
polyphonic, a motet. But how
to sing all the parts? Do you know?

What we are? Perfect
and chaotic and elegant
and ordinary. Elementary
particles, quarks, pieces
in creation's quirkiness.

The striped sea comes
again, again, again. Against
the south wall of the summer
cottage, the drying sunflower
loosens its seeds. They start
falling from the Fibonacci
spirals of their flower-head.

Rain Stories

(one)
The word that comes
after so long an absence, is
bliss. Small moist word.

A two-year-old child
of Australian drought
rolls in a rain puddle
having never seen water
fall from her mother's sky.
In her small fresh life
she had no way of knowing
this bliss is what she wanted.

I have ways of knowing
I am dry. I am wanting
a good hard rain.

(two)
There are two rains I like
to think of as winsomely named
ladies: Serein and Virga.

Serein may have touched you

at dusk in the tropics. So finely
does she fall from a cloudless sky,
you may not have known.

Virga you may have known
as ribbons streaming from clouds,
far off. She evaporates, aloof,
not touching down.

Lady Serein. Lady Virga.

(three)

The only way I know to tell this story is to
call it Rain. Two children visit their grand-
pa's brother, a solitary old man in a small
house by the sea. He once had a wife and
son, but the son, though still alive, was
wasted in Vietnam, and won't come closer
than a ten-foot pole. To the children, the
old man looks like their grandpa. They lean
on his arms, hold hands with him and walk
their bare feet into the sand, asking, telling.
When a squall blows them inside, there's

a tea party at the kitchen table with pack-
aged cookies opened by grandfather-hands.
The old man has long been untouched by a
child's hand. Or any. Children, uninhibited
as rain, don't know the gift they bring. For
the old man, what he didn't know was dry,
is watered. A neglected garden, parched to
the point of unknowing, then a cloudburst:
the children, all talk and touch.

(four)
Driving to Tofino
in the rainstorm, I take the curves
through rivulets cascading onto the road.
They are creeks without names.
There are names without creeks
desert wadis, arroyos,
named and waiting
to be rained into.

You might be waiting too.
To be named. To be filled.

Desert Fathers

Our own deserts are unwanted children,
resented, unembraced. Or, less dramatically,
lost ground, wasted land — dry disgraces
on the way to expected plenitude. Against
our wills, we navigate the shifting grit
blinkered to all but the far, safe side —

       a far cry from the desert fathers
who sought out their austere plots of sand,
determined to sift and mine its very aridity.
Like astronomers quarrying the universe
for dark matter, they followed faint trails
into the desert's shimmering mirages, blistering
days, shivering nights. Sifting, sifting, they
persisted in obedience, stumbling upon agates
of illumination, oblique, like sunlight glancing
off rare oases. They trusted in their shifting
open terrain where something might come clear.
What came clear was their darkness
and the sheer allure of light.

Cloister

The wild and holy
sunshine is segmented

by design, meted out
through stone arcade

to corridor floor: light,
dark, light, dark — graceful

reiteration. Architecture
makes its arguments:

holding something
in, holding something

at bay; shelter,
exposure; simplicity,

intricacy; restraint,
breathing-space; solitude,

engagement; silence,
the breaking of it.

Taking Up the Tracks was previously published in the chapbook *All the Weight She Holds* (Leaf Press, 2013)

The Moon Came in Winter was previously published in the chapbook *A Kind of Mercy* (fearlessPoet Press, 2004)

I Have Never Entered This Barn was previously published in the chapbook *In the Darkness, In the Dream* (Leaf Press, 2012)

Desert Fathers was previously published in *Presence, An International Journal of Spiritual Direction* in September 2006